THE *Fantastic* CUTAWAY BOOK OF RESCUE!

SIMON MUGFORD *AND* ALEX PANG

COPPER BEECH BOOKS
BROOKFIELD, CONNECTICUT

First published in the
United States in 1997 by
Copper Beech Books,
an imprint of
The Millbrook Press
2 Old New Milford Road
Brookfield, Connecticut
06804

Printed in Belgium

Editor
Simon Beecroft
Consultant
Robert Edwards
Design
David West
Children's Book Design
Designer
Robert Perry
Picture research
Brooks Krikler Research
Illustrators
Alex Pang, Ross Watton,
and Mike Saunders

5 4 3 2 1

Library of Congress
Cataloging-in-Publication Data

Mugford, Simon.
The fantastic cutaway book of
rescue / Simon Mugford ;
illustrated by Alex Pang.
p. cm.
Includes index.
Summary: Invites the reader to
peer inside rescue helicopters, fire
engines, submersibles, and other
emergency craft and to find out
how potentially life-threatening
situations are handled.
ISBN 0-7613-0616-1 (lib. bdg.).—
ISBN 0-7613-0630-7 (pbk.)
1. Emergency vehicles—Juvenile
literature. 2. Rescue work—
Juvenile literature. [1.Emergency
vehicles. 2. Rescue work.]
I. Alex Pang, Ross Watton, and
Mike Saunders, ill. II. Title.
TL235.8.M84 1997   97-8022
628.9'2—dc21   CIP AC

CONTENTS

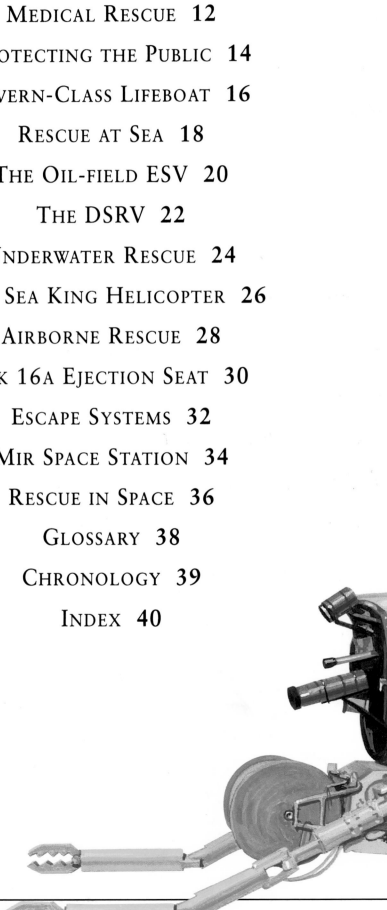

INTRODUCTION

As anyone who has been rescued from a capsized boat, a craggy mountainside, or a burning building knows – there is nothing like the sight of a rescue worker when you are in trouble. Emergencies and disasters can occur anywhere, from submarines at the bottom of the sea to spacecraft in space – and specialized vehicles, equipment, and techniques have been developed to cope in almost any environment. The use of communication technology, such as radar and satellites, has made the location of people in peril easier. Yet however advanced the technology, the role played by highly trained individuals, who often risk their own lives to save others, is still perhaps the most impressive aspect of any emergency situation. Rescue is often a highly dangerous activity, which calls for a high degree of human ingenuity, expertise, and bravery.

IF AN AIRCRAFT catches fire on the runway, burning fuel can engulf it within a few minutes. A specially designed fire truck like this one, stationed close to the runway, can cover the runway with foam even before a distressed plane has landed. These high-performance trucks can accelerate from 0-50 mph (0-80 km/h) in 20 seconds, to a top speed of 87 mph (140 km/h). A major incident will require several such trucks, plus support vehicles. Airports maintain rigorous safety procedures, and firefighting technology is being continuously developed to reduce the response time to incidents.

FOAM, WATER, AND POWDER

An airport crash truck carries a combination of water, foam, and chemical powders. A typical truck will have 2,113 gallons (8,000 liters) of water. It also has 264 gallons (1,000 liters) of foam to smother fuel fires.

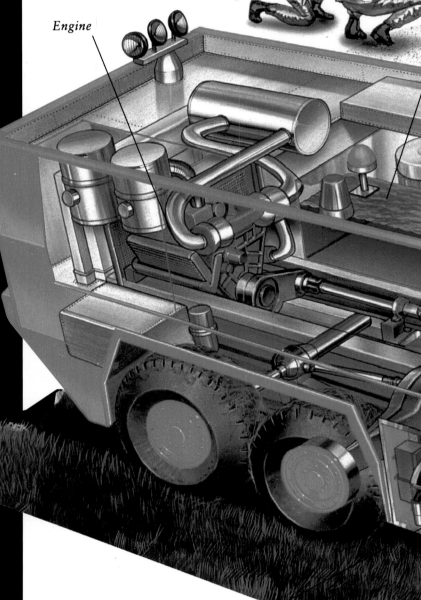

Engine

Foam tank

Equipment, including hoses, ladders, and breathing apparatus

A BURNING AIRCRAFT IS SMOTHERED IN FOAM

EXTINGUISHING THE FIRE

There is one foam cannon situated on the top of the cab, and another two under the front bumper for extinguishing fires on the ground. They can pump all the truck's supply of foam and water onto the fire in about 20 seconds.

Foam cannon

Cab

FIRE CREW
Airport firefighters may have to work at night under floodlights as they assist in evacuating passengers and crew from the aircraft. The workers are protected from the heat by heat-resistant aluminum suits.

EIGHT-WHEEL DRIVE
All eight wheels are used to drive the truck. This helps it to accelerate quickly and maintain its grip on the runway, which may be slippery with oil and water.

AIRPORT CRASH TRUCK

FIREFIGHTING VEHICLES

*T*he first fire engines, made in around 1800, were pumped by hand. The Sutherland Steam Fire Engine (left) is an early horse-drawn fire engine. It was one of the first engines to have a steam pump, which could pump water to a height of 160 ft (48 m). The Sutherland won an international competition in Crystal Palace, London, in 1863. Modern firefighting vehicles can discharge much greater amounts of foam or water. Specially designed vehicles can reach people in tall buildings and can travel in confined spaces; for example, along underground train tunnels and in very narrow streets.

DENNIS FIRE PUMP

This Dennis Fire Pump (below) was used by the London Fire Brigade in 1934. It was one of the first vehicles to carry a ladder long enough to reach the top of tall buildings. There was little protection for its crew of four. Sometimes, firefighters were seriously injured, or even killed, when they were flung from the truck as it sped to a fire.

Winch, for raising ladder

Water tank

Ladder

Hose

ALL-TERRAIN FIRE FIGHTER

The Hagglunds Bv206 (left) is designed for wartime use. It carries out fire and rescue operations in inaccessible areas, and can be lifted by helicopter. The vehicle can pump 150 gallons (682 liters) of foam a minute, and its crew are equipped with cutters, saws, and lifting bags.

Cab

Equipment (first-aid kit, fire extinguishers, breathing apparatus, and stretchers)

Foam tank

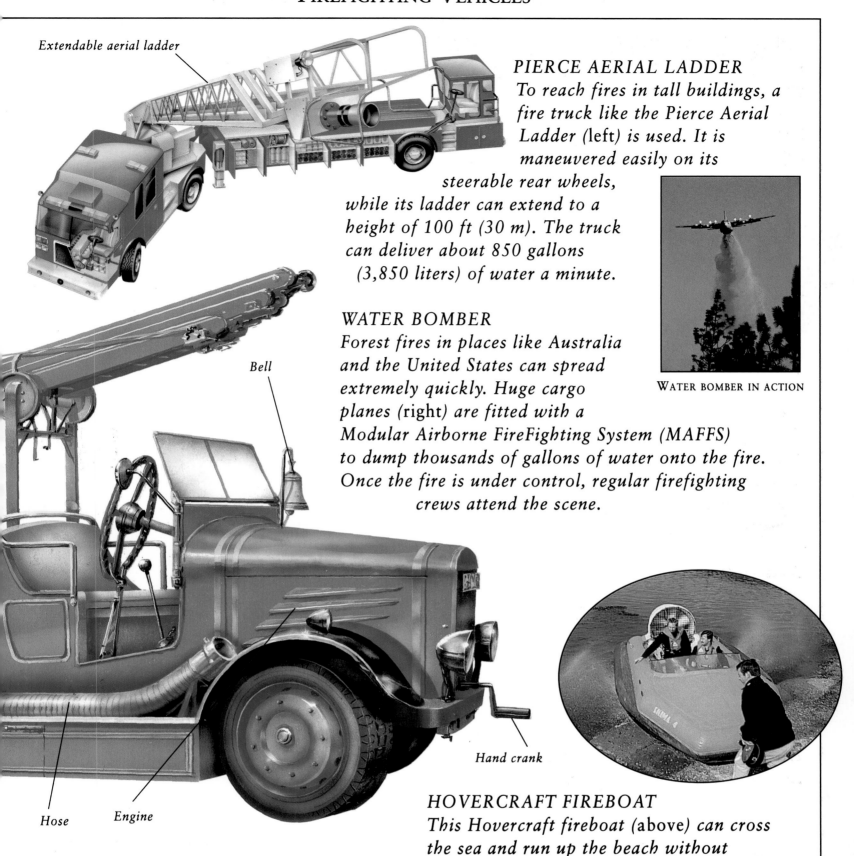

Extendable aerial ladder

Bell

Hose   Engine

Hand crank

PIERCE AERIAL LADDER

To reach fires in tall buildings, a fire truck like the Pierce Aerial Ladder (left) is used. It is maneuvered easily on its steerable rear wheels, while its ladder can extend to a height of 100 ft (30 m). The truck can deliver about 850 gallons (3,850 liters) of water a minute.

WATER BOMBER IN ACTION

WATER BOMBER

Forest fires in places like Australia and the United States can spread extremely quickly. Huge cargo planes (right) are fitted with a Modular Airborne FireFighting System (MAFFS) to dump thousands of gallons of water onto the fire. Once the fire is under control, regular firefighting crews attend the scene.

HOVERCRAFT FIREBOAT

This Hovercraft fireboat (above) can cross the sea and run up the beach without stopping, as well as travel over flat terrain.

CHANNEL TUNNEL STTS

This Service Tunnel Transport System (STTS, right) attends to emergencies and fires in the Channel Tunnel, which links Britain and France. It can be driven in both directions – automatically, if necessary – and carries hoses, breathing apparatus, and cutting gear. Passengers can be carried in the middle of the vehicle.

STTS FIRE ENGINE USED IN THE CHANNEL TUNNEL

THE FIREFIGHTERS

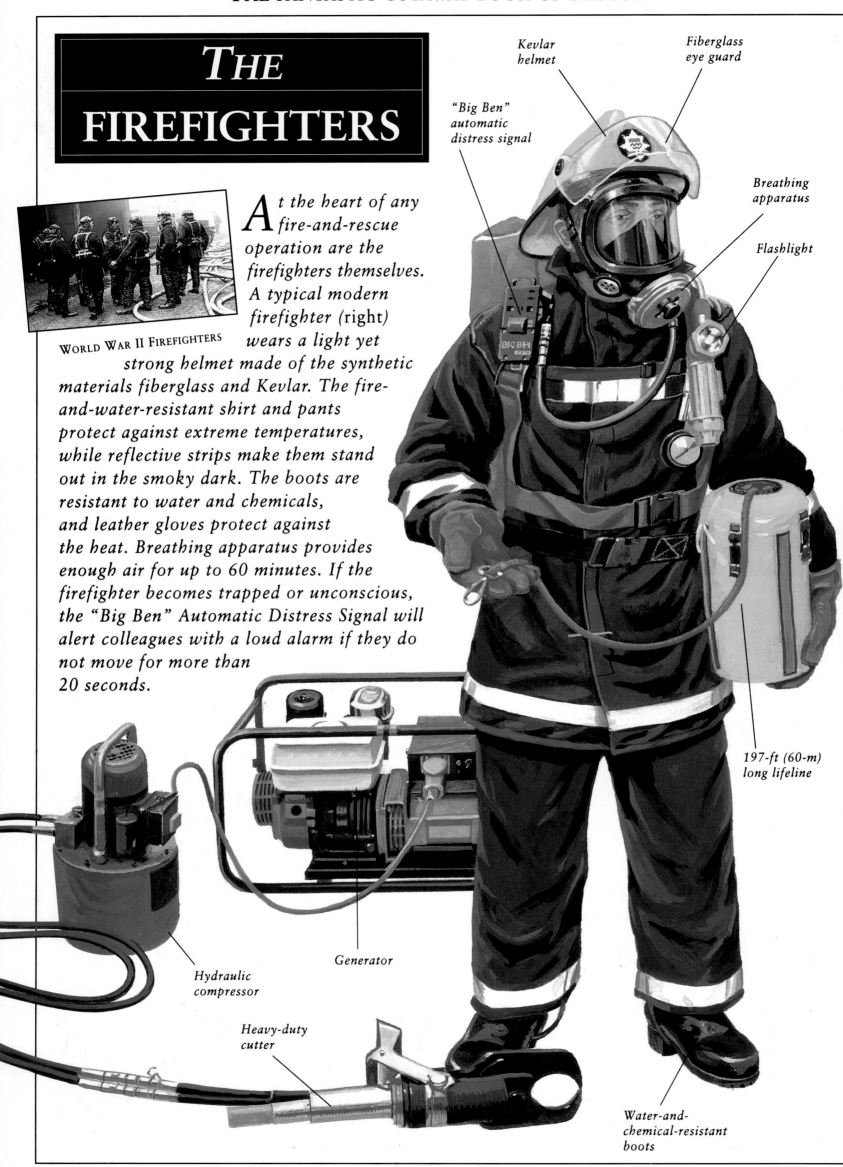

WORLD WAR II FIREFIGHTERS

*A*t the heart of any fire-and-rescue operation are the firefighters themselves. A typical modern firefighter (right) wears a light yet strong helmet made of the synthetic materials fiberglass and Kevlar. The fire-and-water-resistant shirt and pants protect against extreme temperatures, while reflective strips make them stand out in the smoky dark. The boots are resistant to water and chemicals, and leather gloves protect against the heat. Breathing apparatus provides enough air for up to 60 minutes. If the firefighter becomes trapped or unconscious, the "Big Ben" Automatic Distress Signal will alert colleagues with a loud alarm if they do not move for more than 20 seconds.

Kevlar helmet

Fiberglass eye guard

"Big Ben" automatic distress signal

Breathing apparatus

Flashlight

197-ft (60-m) long lifeline

Hydraulic compressor

Generator

Heavy-duty cutter

Water-and-chemical-resistant boots

TRAPPED

Firefighters do not only put out fires. They may also be called to a wide range of incidents, including rescuing people trapped in elevators and vehicles, making structures safe, and controlling spills of flammable or toxic liquids. In France, firefighters, called pompiers, are called in to all types of emergencies and are also trained as paramedics. These firefighters are rescuing someone trapped in a cave (above).

FIREFIGHTERS AT A CAVE RESCUE

TRAINING

All firefighters undergo extensive training to make them physically and mentally strong enough to deal with difficult situations.

WATER-HOSE PRACTICE

A firefighter spends up to 20 weeks in training before being assigned to a post. They experience "real fire" conditions in smoke and heat rooms, and practice dealing with conditions such as flooded basements. They learn first-aid and rescue techniques using a range of specialized equipment. Some knowledge, however, can only be gained during real situations.

RAIL DISASTERS

DERAILED AMTRAK TRAIN

Train crashes present firefighters with a difficult and harrowing task. A typical rail disaster is likely to involve several hundred people, and the firefighters must work closely with the other emergency services to ensure that survivors are rescued as quickly and safely as possible. In September 1992, this Amtrak train was derailed on a bridge and crashed into a swamp near Mobile, Alabama (left). The rescue operation was made even more challenging because the swamp was full of alligators, which attacked and ate some of the passengers!

THERMAL-IMAGING EQUIPMENT

Thermal imaging, or infrared equipment, is an extremely useful tool for the modern firefighter. By detecting heat, it can be used to locate people trapped under rubble. Specially trained "sniffer" dogs may be involved in the search as well. The latest thermal-imaging equipment is helmet-mounted and can detect people at distances of up to 1,640 ft (500 m). Thermal imagers also are used to pinpoint a fire's "hotspot," or hottest area.

FIREFIGHTERS USING THERMAL-IMAGING EQUIPMENT

LIFESAVING EQUIPMENT

Like most emergency medical vehicles, "Bigfoot" carries a range of special medical equipment. There is a cardiac monitor to keep a check on a patient's heart and a defibrillator, an electrical device used to restart a patient's heart if it stops beating. There are also supplies of oxygen, medicine, and blankets.

FIELD HOSPITAL

For major incidents, where a number of casualties require treatment, "Bigfoot" carries an inflatable tent to provide a mini-hospital. This is attached to the side of the vehicle. It can be secured to the ground by sandbags or stakes.

OFF-ROAD MODIFICATIONS

"Bigfoot" is specially modified to allow it to cross difficult terrain. The chassis is raised to allow more clearance between the ground and the vehicle, and special tires help it to grip muddy and slippery roads and tracks.

Field hospital

Cardiac monitor

"BIGFOOT" RACES TO THE SCENE OF AN ACCIDENT

WHEN A SERIOUS ACCIDENT occurs in open countryside or along a railroad track, ordinary ambulances may not be able to reach the incident. This specially-modified Renault Messenger is a

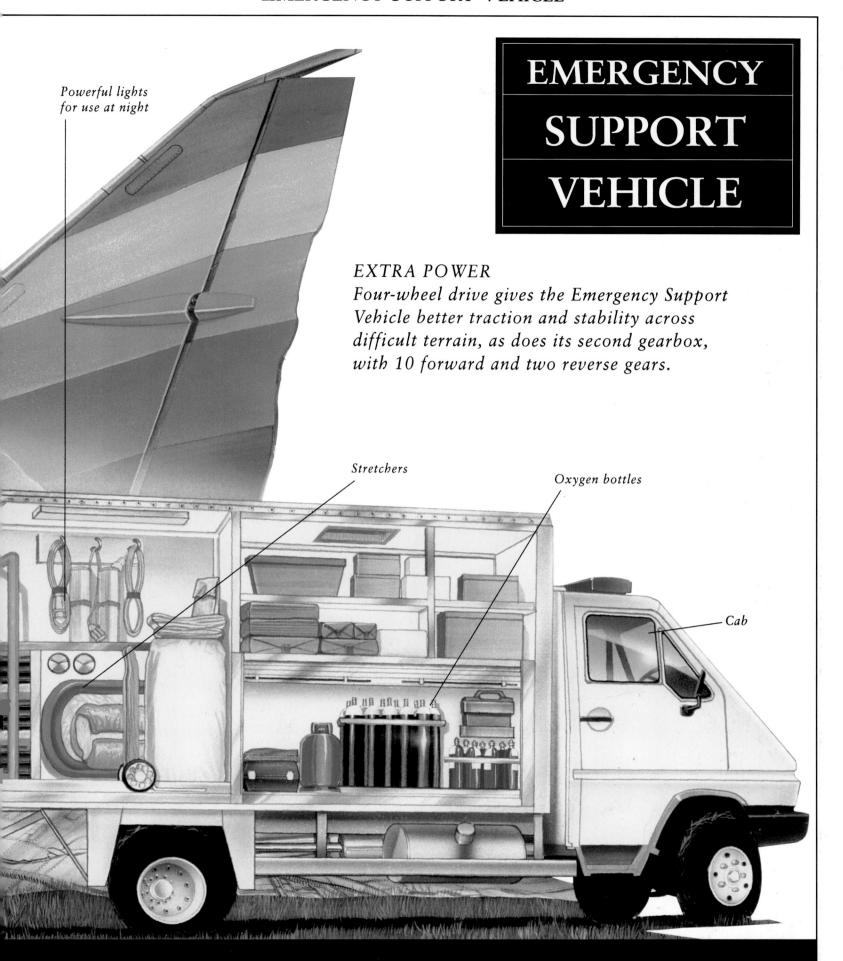

Powerful lights
for use at night

EMERGENCY SUPPORT VEHICLE

EXTRA POWER
Four-wheel drive gives the Emergency Support
Vehicle better traction and stability across
difficult terrain, as does its second gearbox,
with 10 forward and two reverse gears.

Stretchers

Oxygen bottles

Cab

medical Emergency Support Vehicle (ESV), nicknamed "Bigfoot." It attends to patients and carries supplies and a range of specialized equipment to incidents in hard-to-reach places. A 2.5-liter turbo diesel engine powers the vehicle. Paramedics are trained to transport patients across difficult and bumpy conditions, and regular ambulances then complete the journey to hospital.

MEDICAL RESCUE

AMBULANCE AT SEA

Offshore powerboats race at speeds up to 120 knots (136 mph). In case of accident, marine ambulances are in attendance at races. These fast craft take doctors and paramedics to the scene of an accident very quickly, where the injured driver can be treated on the spot (below).

OFFSHORE POWERBOAT ACCIDENT

Since ancient Roman times, wagons have been used to transport the sick and injured – they were commonly used on battlefields. The first motorized ambulances were introduced in 1902. This ambulance train (left) was used by the British Army in France during World War I. Today, medical emergency vehicles carry specialized equipment. Paramedics, like this one in Japan (right), attend to patients at the scene of the accident and on the way to the hospital.

A PARAMEDIC IN JAPAN

PARAMEDIC MOTORCYCLE

Congested city streets make it difficult for ambulances to get to an accident scene quickly: Paramedics on motorcycles cut down response times. This Honda ST1100 (below left) is specially built for emergency situations. Its medical equipment includes a machine for recording patients' blood pressure, a heart monitor and defibrillator, an oxygen cylinder, and a stethoscope.

Telescopic flashing light

Blankets

Windshield

First-aid kit

Cardiac monitor and defibrillator

Radial tire

Reflective markings

HONDA ST1100 MOTORCYCLE

AIR AMBULANCE

*The Helicopter Emergency
Service (HEMS, right) is cleared to
land anywhere in London – such
as in a street or on the top of
a building. It flies at over
200 mph (320 km/h) and can
reach any part of the city
within 10 minutes. On average, it
is called out three times a day and
saves about 12 lives a year.*

FORMULA ONE

*Racing car drivers
involved in accidents may be
so seriously injured that they need major
medical attention immediately. A mobile hospital
like this (below) is used to treat them. It has its
own generators to power an operating theater,
an examination room to treat minor injuries,
a defibrillator, and a refrigerated blood bank.*

Examination
room

Emergency
operating
theater

Cab

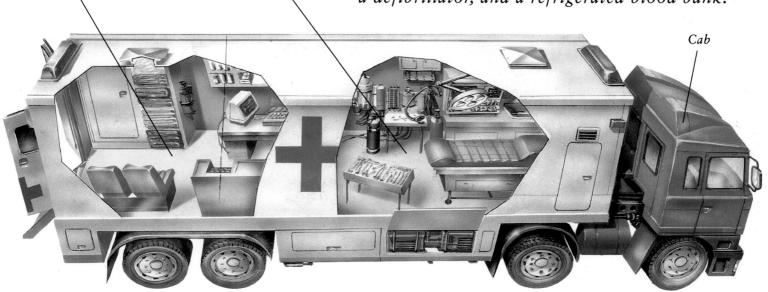

MOBILE HOSPITAL

MOUNTAIN RESCUE

*The equipment carried by
mountain rescue teams (right)
includes first aid, flares, a
radio, food, survival bags, and
stretchers. Mountain rescuers
must be experienced climbers,
as they often need to climb to
an injured person. They carry
equipment for climbing, such as
ice axes, ropes, and harnesses.*

MEDICAL EQUIPMENT USED IN MOUNTAIN RESCUE

PROTECTING THE PUBLIC

SWAT TEAM IN THE UNITED STATES

Terrorist activity poses a threat to many countries around the world. In June 1996, the city center of Manchester, Britain was wrecked by a bomb (left). The bomb had been planted by the Irish Republican Army (IRA), who want the reunification of Ireland. Bomb-disposal experts try to disarm terrorist bombs from a safe distance using equipment like this robot (below). It is radio-controlled and has closed-circuit T.V. equipment. Antiterrorism teams are usually secretive organizations because of the dangerous nature of their work.

SWAT VAN

Many police forces in the United States have dedicated Special Weapons And Tactics (SWAT) teams to end sieges. Heavily armed vehicles like this one (above) are used in such situations, while British riot police use armored vans (below). Unusual or very dangerous situations require highly trained individuals. The British Special Air Service (SAS) and U.S. commandos have been involved in military hostage situations around the world.

BRITISH RIOT POLICE VANS

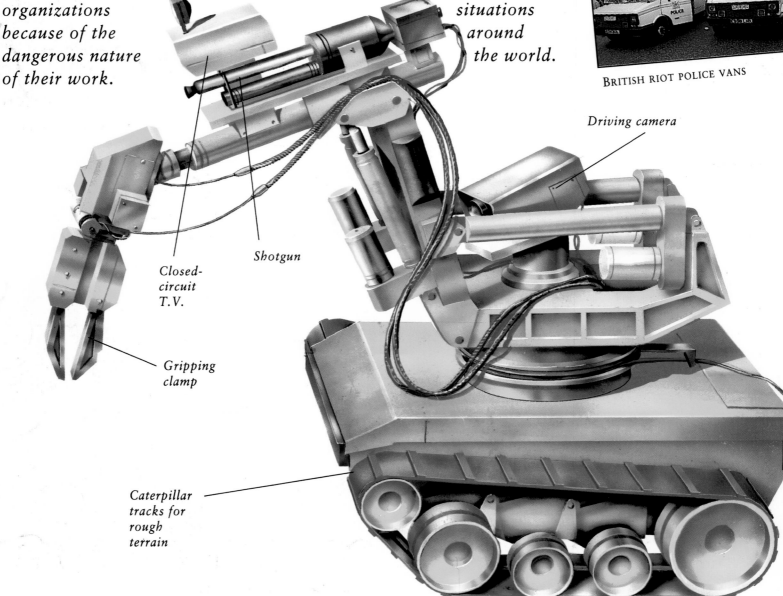

Driving camera

Shotgun

Closed-circuit T.V.

Gripping clamp

Caterpillar tracks for rough terrain

MAV 5 LIGHT ARMORED VEHICLE

This armored vehicle, used in Italy, can carry six crew members into situations where they may encounter heavy gunfire. An all-terrain vehicle, the MAV 5 is protected by armored steel, 0.2 in (6 mm) thick. It has a system to protect the crew from tear gas, and can act as an ambulance, mobile first-aid, repair, and recovery unit.

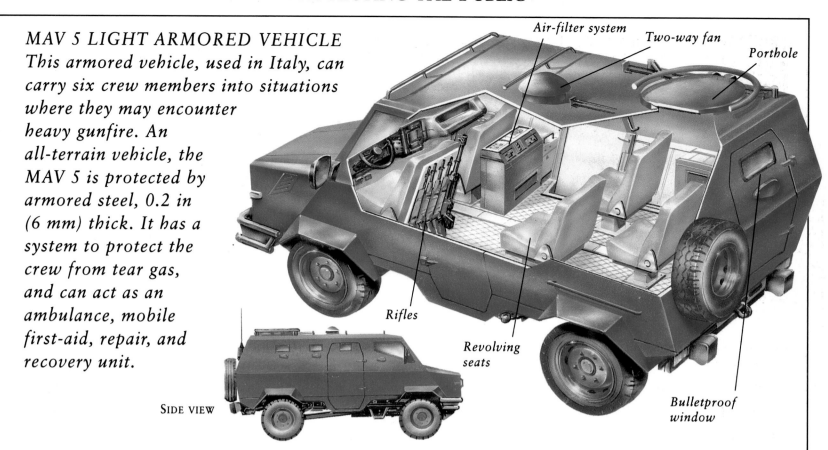

Air-filter system

Two-way fan

Porthole

Rifles

Revolving seats

Bulletproof window

SIDE VIEW

EMERGENCY RESPONSE UNIT

UNDERGROUND EMERGENCY

Accidents in an underground subway system are attended by all emergency services, but specialized equipment is needed for some operations. Some subway systems provide an emergency response unit (left) to deal with collisions and derailments, people trapped under trains, and flooded tunnels. The unit is used at major incidents to coordinate the rescue operation.

EQUIPMENT CARRIED BY THE VEHICLE

HOSTAGE RESCUE

In April 1997, 71 hostages were freed from the Japanese Ambassador's residence in Lima, the capital of Peru. The hostages had been held there for four months by a revolutionary movement. More than 100 commandos stormed the residence after tunneling underneath and blasting the area where the rebels were hiding (far right). The commandos were trained in the United States by FBI agents (right). All of the rebels were killed, but only one of the hostages died.

A COMMANDO EMERGES FROM A TUNNEL

SEVERN-CLASS LIFEBOAT

CREW MEMBERS

The crew of six elect a coxswain, who is in charge of the boat. The crew also train volunteers, who must be willing to risk their own lives to save others. Sometimes a doctor will travel on board as well.

RIGHTING ITSELF

Because lifeboats often work in rough conditions, there is a high risk of capsizing (turning upside down in the water). The Severn's hull is designed so that if this should happen, it can turn itself upright within a few minutes.

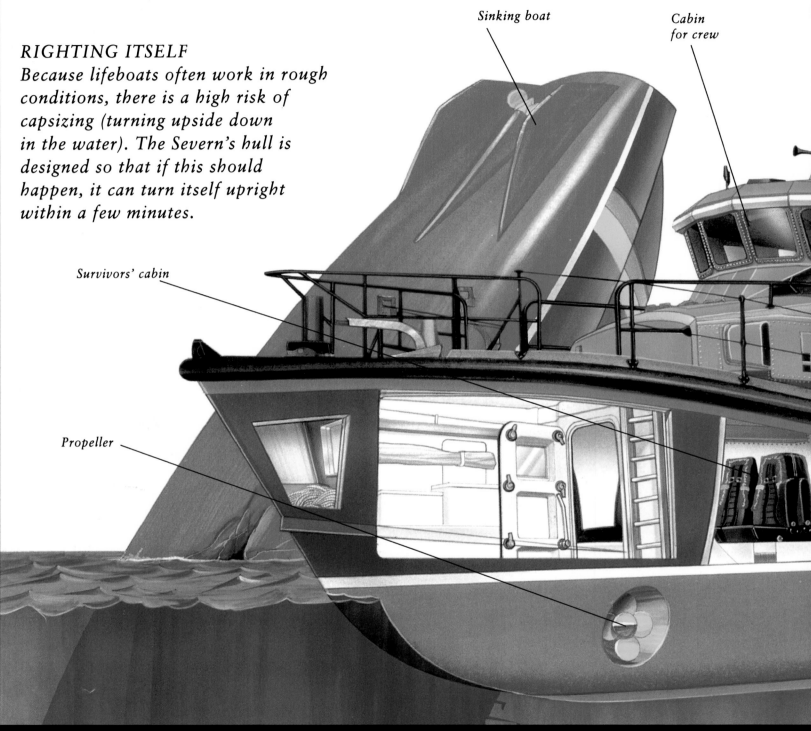

Sinking boat

Cabin for crew

Survivors' cabin

Propeller

A LIFEBOAT CREW ON THEIR WAY TO AN EMERGENCY

DISASTERS AT SEA can happen in the worst of weather conditions, and a lifeboat such as this Severn-Class would play a major role in a large, offshore rescue operation. The Severn, at a length of 55 ft (17 m), is the largest and newest lifeboat operated

Navigation equipment

MAKING ROOM
A passenger ferry can carry hundreds of passengers. If necessary, the Severn can carry up to 200 survivors.

SMALL INFLATABLE
In the event of an emergency close to shore, the Severn carries a small, Y-class inflatable, launched from the side (or rear) of the boat, which can travel quickly in shallow water.

RESCUE WINCH IN OPERATION

Cabin

LIFE JACKETS
Spending longer than a few minutes in cold water can be fatal, and the life jackets carried on board are used to haul people out of the water as quickly as possible.

by the Royal National Lifeboat Institution (RNLI) in Britain. With a maximum speed of 25 knots (28 mph), it is designed to skim across the surface of the water to get to the scene of an emergency as quickly as possible.

It carries the latest navigation technology, including charts stored on CD-ROM. Major rescue missions are coordinated by coast guards, and may also include the use of a helicopter such as a Sea King (*see* pages 26-27).

RESCUE AT SEA

U.S. COAST GUARD

*C*oast guards, often working with naval and air forces, coordinate maritime rescues, carry out environmental patrols and clean-up operations, and, in some countries, are involved in pursuing drug smugglers, pirates, and illegal immigrants. Coast guard operations often use airplanes and helicopters (see pages 28-29). They also work with a wide range of sea vessels, from small, fast inflatable craft to 140-ft (42-m) long ice-breaking tugs (below), each designed for a specific task. Sea-rescue operations are likely to become easier as navigation and satellite positioning equipment improves, making stranded mariners easier to locate.

CAPSIZED BOAT
The growing popularity of sailing and other water sports causes more emergencies to occur. In this case (below), survivors are attempting to escape to an inflatable life raft. The life raft has a canopy over the top to provide shelter from the cold. It also has emergency supplies and first-aid equipment.

SAIL BOAT RESCUE

TASKFORCE 1100
Many of the world's airports are situated close to the sea, and the Taskforce 1100 (below) is designed to provide a rapid response should an incident occur in or close to the water. It is propelled by water jets and has a shallow draft, which allows it to travel at up to 28 knots (32 mph) in very shallow water. Firefighting equipment and life rafts for 420 people are carried onboard, and the boat acts as a communication center until larger vessels arrive.

TASKFORCE 1100

Ice-breaking hull

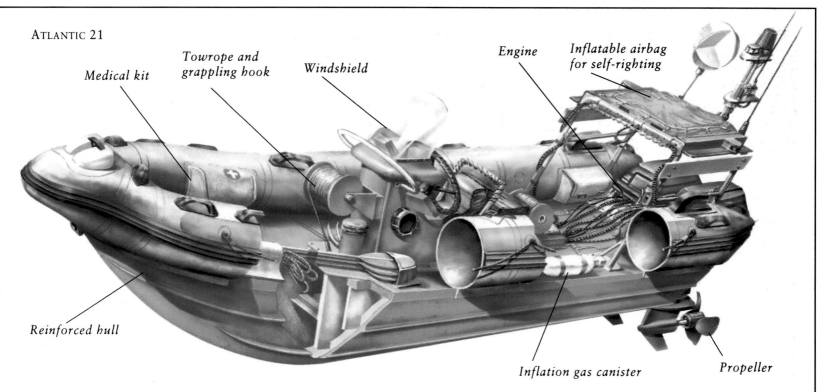

ATLANTIC 21

Medical kit

Towrope and grappling hook

Windshield

Engine

Inflatable airbag for self-righting

Reinforced hull

Inflation gas canister

Propeller

ATLANTIC 21

The Atlantic 21 (above) is a semi-rigid inflatable craft used for operations close to the shore. Capable of speeds of up to 29 knots (34 mph), it responds quickly to incidents involving people who may be stranded on rocks or in shallow water. The crew carry basic first-aid and rescue equipment. If the craft capsizes, an airbag inflates to turn it upright.

AUSTRALIAN LIFEGUARDS RIDE THE WAVES!

SURFBOAT

This boat is used by lifeguards off the coast of Australia. Its hull is specially designed to cope with the huge, rolling surf in these waters. Lifeguards also use a surfboard-style boat to make quick rescues.

TUGBOAT

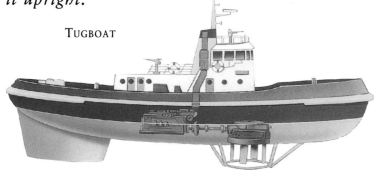

FERRY DISASTER

LARGE-SCALE DISASTERS

In 1987, the Herald of Free Enterprise ferry toppled over when water swamped through the bow doors. A 24-hour rescue operation took place (right), with boats, helicopters, and 30 ambulances.

OIL-TANKER ON FIRE

Damaged oil tankers also need immediate emergency attention because oil spills are very hazardous (above). Crippled vessels are towed by tugs (above top), which can pull as much as 93 tons each.

OIL FIELDS can be situated many miles out to sea, making it necessary for emergency and rescue services to be permanently located nearby. Oil-field Emergency Support Vessels (ESVs) are huge floating platforms used to put out fires, rescue people, and make burning oil wells safe. They provide a mobile base for helicopters, inflatable craft, and diving teams. A typical ESV carries a crew of 95 people including medical staff, firefighters, and engineers. Massive diesel engines are used to propel the ESV to a speed of 12 knots (14 mph). Lifeboats and other safety equipment are on board should the ESV itself get in trouble.

AN ESV TACKLES A FIRE ON AN OIL RIG

FIGHTING FIRES

The ESV is itself a firefighting vessel. Up to 17 water guns are positioned at various points on the vessel. These can pump 50,000 gallons (227,500 liters) of water a minute onto the fire from up to 590 ft (180 m) away. Foam stored in the corner columns is used to smother burning oil. If the ESV gets too close to the fire and endangers the crew, a sprinkler system on board will douse the platform itself with water.

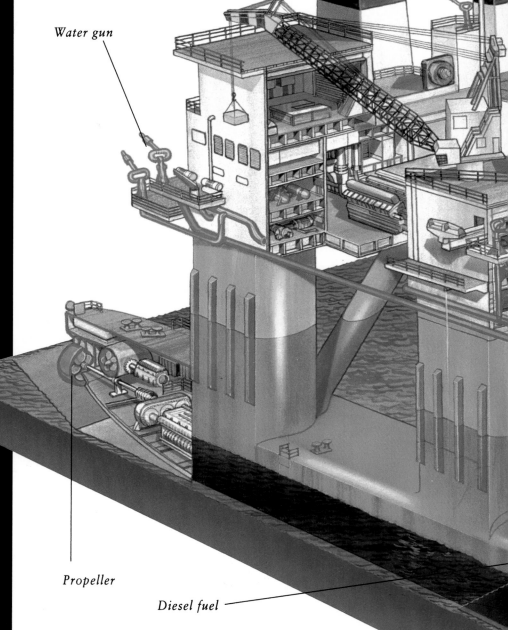

Water gun

Propeller

Diesel fuel

CONTROLLING THE ESV

Like a normal ship, the ESV is controlled from the heavily protected bridge on the upper deck. Propulsion comes from propellers at the rear of each of its two hulls. Computer-controlled thrusters situated in the sides of the hull let the ESV turn sideways and remain stationary without dropping anchor.

HELICOPTERS AND INFLATABLES

A helicopter, such as a Sea King (see page 26-27), is kept on board to rescue survivors from the oil platform or water. They also provide support for the three or four fast inflatable boats, which are lowered into the water by crane.

THE OIL-FIELD ESV

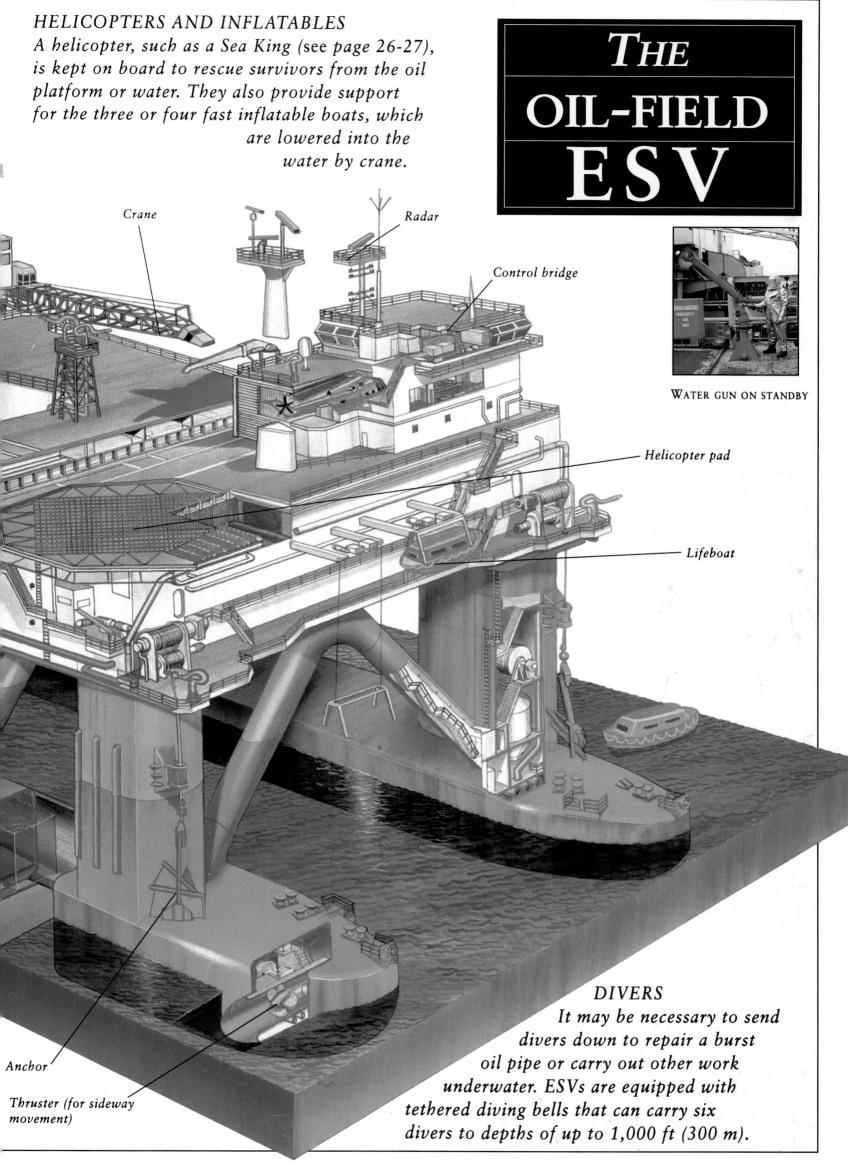

WATER GUN ON STANDBY

Crane

Radar

Control bridge

Helicopter pad

Lifeboat

Anchor

Thruster (for sideway movement)

DIVERS

It may be necessary to send divers down to repair a burst oil pipe or carry out other work underwater. ESVs are equipped with tethered diving bells that can carry six divers to depths of up to 1,000 ft (300 m).

IN THE EVENT of a submarine becoming disabled underwater, only another submarine will be able to carry out a successful rescue operation. The Deep Submergence Rescue Vehicle (DSRV) is designed to be put into action quickly anywhere around the world. It can be transported by road, aircraft, ship, or specially modified submarine. The DSRV is 49 ft (15 m) long and can operate to a depth of 5,000 ft (1,500 m). It is designed to work in all conditions, and, if necessary, can carry out a rescue operation under the ice. There are currently two DSRVs in operation: *Avalon* and *Mystic*. They are both based at the U.S. Naval base in San Diego, California.

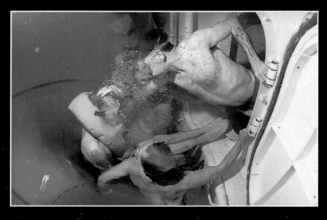

SUBMARINE RESCUE

CARRIED PIGGYBACK STYLE

When a submarine is in trouble, the DSRV is taken to the nearest port and attached, piggyback style, to a "parent" submarine. This provides an underwater base: The DSRV carries up to 24 survivors at a time between the disabled craft and the parent submarine.

Distressed submarine

CONTROLLING THE DSRV

The pilot and copilot operate the DSRV from the forward-most of the three inner spheres. Special mercury sensors are used to help keep the DSRV from tilting and rolling too far.

ELECTRONIC EYES AND EARS

The DSRV uses sonar to detect stricken craft and find its depth. Sonar sends out sound waves, which bounce off objects and are returned as "echoes." These echoes tell the crew how far away objects are. Cameras are used to pinpoint the exact position of the disabled submarine and to find its escape hatches.

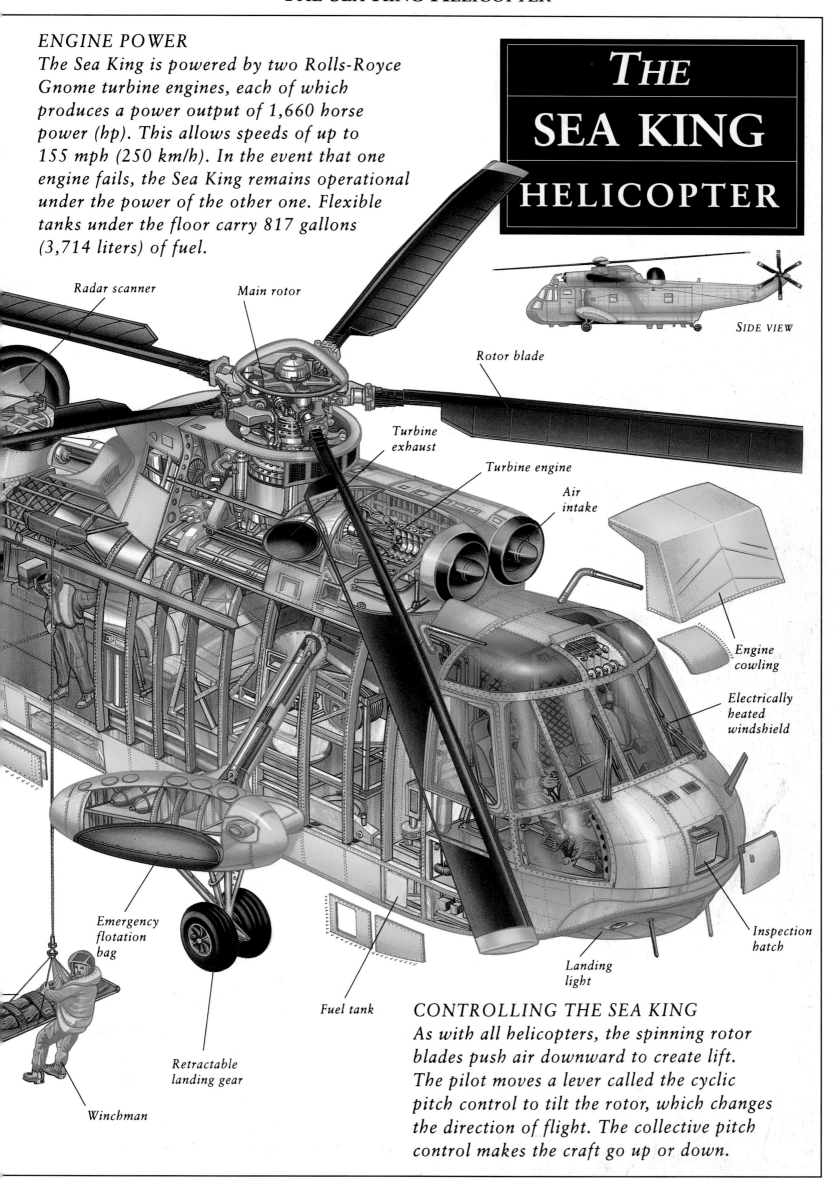

ENGINE POWER

The Sea King is powered by two Rolls-Royce Gnome turbine engines, each of which produces a power output of 1,660 horse power (hp). This allows speeds of up to 155 mph (250 km/h). In the event that one engine fails, the Sea King remains operational under the power of the other one. Flexible tanks under the floor carry 817 gallons (3,714 liters) of fuel.

THE SEA KING HELICOPTER

SIDE VIEW

Radar scanner

Main rotor

Rotor blade

Turbine exhaust

Turbine engine

Air intake

Engine cowling

Electrically heated windshield

Emergency flotation bag

Inspection hatch

Landing light

Winchman

Retractable landing gear

Fuel tank

CONTROLLING THE SEA KING

As with all helicopters, the spinning rotor blades push air downward to create lift. The pilot moves a lever called the cyclic pitch control to tilt the rotor, which changes the direction of flight. The collective pitch control makes the craft go up or down.

AIRBORNE RESCUE

FLYING DOC
The Royal Flying
Doctor Service
in Australia is an
airborne medical
service for the
outback, a huge

A WELCOME SIGHT – THE FLYING DOCTOR!

area of desert covering about 2.7 million sq
miles (7 million sq km). Receiving emergency
calls from remote communities, the 38
aircraft make about 82 flights every day
of the year.

TROOPS BEING EVACUATED DURING THE VIETNAM WAR

On land or at sea, airplanes and
helicopters play a crucial role in rescue
missions. In wartime, a large helicopter like
the Chinook is used to get troops out of
dangerous situations (above). The
Chinook is the workhorse
of air forces around the
world: It has a range
of 580 miles
(935 km) and
can be refueled
in mid air.

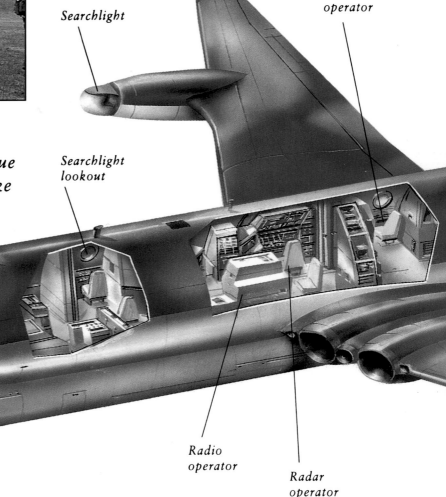

Searchlight

MAD
operator

Searchlight
lookout

Radar
scanner

Radio
operator

Radar
operator

LYNX HELICOPTER
The Lynx helicopter is often used for military
search-and-rescue missions. Originally

Thermal imager

designed for anti-
submarine activities, it
is fast and very
maneuverable, capable
of 249 mph (400 km/h).
In poor visibility the Lynx
uses sophisticated Marconi
Sea Owl thermal-imaging
equipment to locate
survivors.

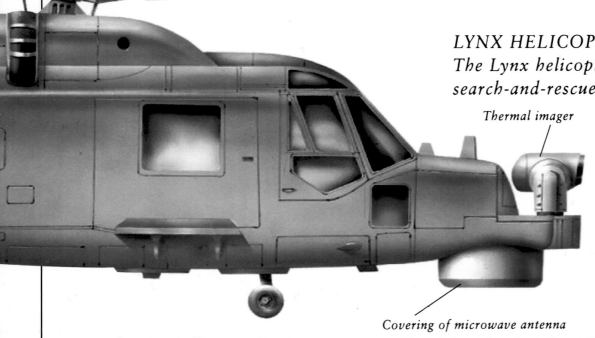

Covering of microwave antenna

MOUNTAIN RESCUE
In mountainous areas, avalanches, can trap skiers and mountain climbers, and sometimes devastate mountainside villages. This firefighting team in Japan is involved in mountain rescue, and carries equipment in its helicopters for almost any situation (right).

EQUIPMENT USED IN MOUNTAIN RESCUE

Sonar buoy storage

MAD boom

Sonar buoy launcher

NIMROD
The British Nimrod (left) is used for long-range rescue missions, sometimes thousands of miles out to sea. It carries a range of sophisticated search and tracking equipment, including MAD (magnetic anomaly detector) technology, which detects submarines using a long boom, or pole, attached to the plane's tail. The Nimrod also drops sonar buoys below the water to fix a submarine's position and speed. The Nimrod's typical range is 5,755 miles (9,265 km), but, if necessary, it can save fuel by flying on only one of its four engines.

External fuel tank

FLARECRAFT SKIMS OVER THE WATER

FLARECRAFT
Some experimental craft, like this Flarecraft L-325 (right), use "ground effect" to create a cushion of air that allows them to skim over the surface of the water. They can travel at speeds up to 160 knots (186 mph), and are much more efficient than normal hovercraft. These craft are potentially very useful for rescue work.

A PILOT EJECTS FROM A BURNING PLANE

THE EUROFIGHTER 2000 is a state-of-the-art fighter jet, intended to replace the aging Tornado fighter in the near future. It is packed with an incredible array of technology, but the most important safety feature is the ejector seat. Ejection seats produced by the Martin-Baker company have saved more than 6,000 lives since the 1940s, and the Mk 16A has been designed especially for the Eurofighter 2000. Like the Eurofighter jet, the ejector seat is very light; it weighs less than the pilot, and can operate at altitudes of up to 50,000 ft (15,240 m).

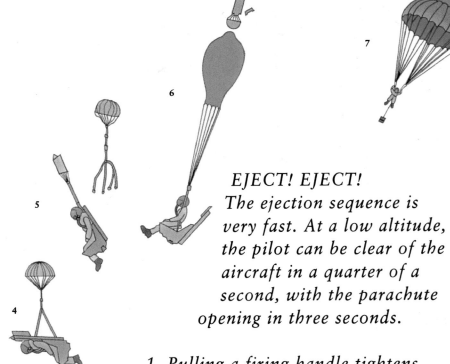

EJECT! EJECT!
The ejection sequence is very fast. At a low altitude, the pilot can be clear of the aircraft in a quarter of a second, with the parachute opening in three seconds.

1 *Pulling a firing handle tightens the seat straps, and the roof of the cockpit is fired away.*

2 *Emergency radio and oxygen supply are activated, and the seat is fired up the guide rails and free of the plane by the ejection gun.*

3 *The rocket thrusters fire the seat about 330 ft (100 m) away from the plane.*

4 *The first parachute is released, which helps to stabilize and slow the seat down.*

5 *The first parachute is detached.*

6 *At the right altitude, the main parachute is deployed, and the pilot is pulled from the seat.*

7 *A personal locator beacon is activated and the pilot parachutes to the ground.*

A PILOT TESTS AN EJECTION SEAT

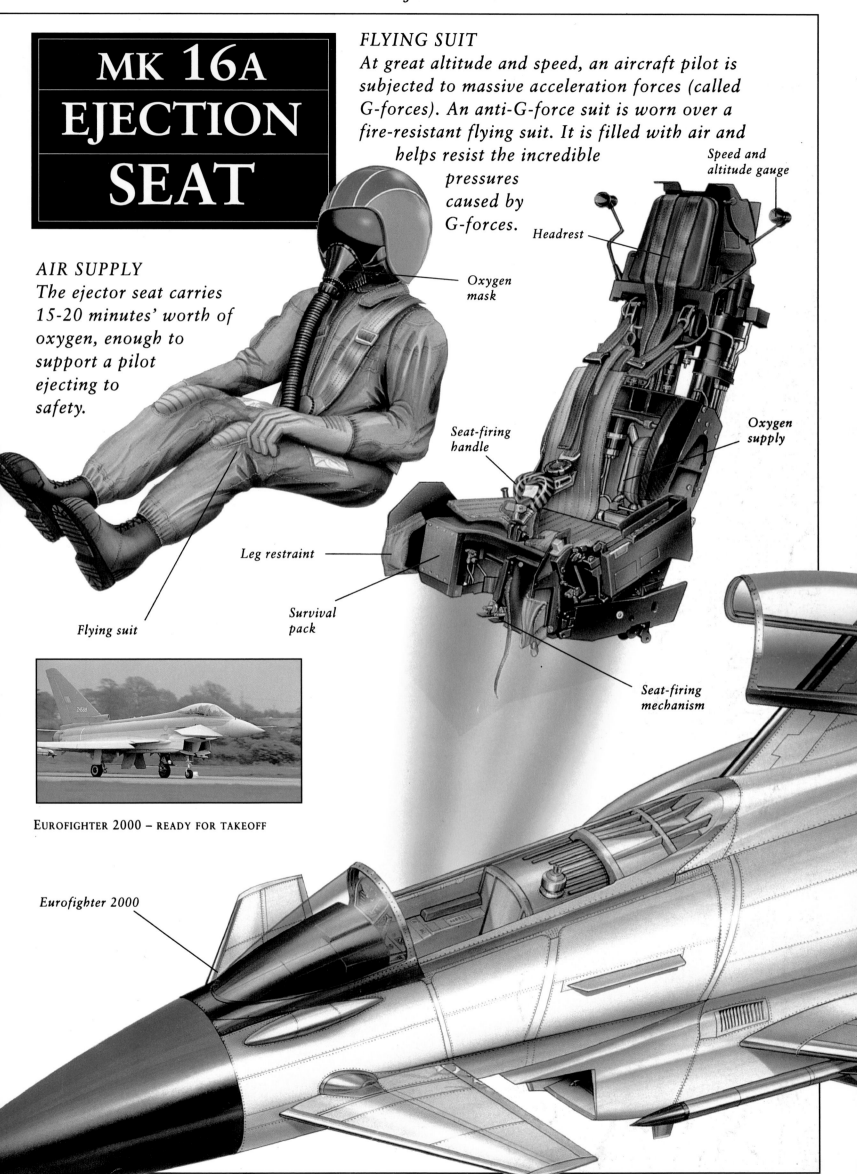

MK 16A EJECTION SEAT

FLYING SUIT
At great altitude and speed, an aircraft pilot is subjected to massive acceleration forces (called G-forces). An anti-G-force suit is worn over a fire-resistant flying suit. It is filled with air and helps resist the incredible pressures caused by G-forces.

Speed and altitude gauge

Headrest

Oxygen mask

AIR SUPPLY
The ejector seat carries 15-20 minutes' worth of oxygen, enough to support a pilot ejecting to safety.

Seat-firing handle

Oxygen supply

Leg restraint

Survival pack

Flying suit

Seat-firing mechanism

EUROFIGHTER 2000 – READY FOR TAKEOFF

Eurofighter 2000

31

ESCAPE SYSTEMS

PROPELLED OUT OF DANGER

*I*n some situations either there is not enough time to wait to be rescued, or rescue is technically impossible. Pilots of supersonic aircraft flying at high altitudes need to be able to eject very quickly to save themselves (left), and many types of ejection seat have been developed for different aircraft. Escape systems have also been manufactured for a range of other vehicles, including spacecraft, boats, and submarines.

MARINE EMERGENCY CHUTE

To evacuate the passengers and crew from stricken ships, inflatable emergency chutes are used to transfer people to the life rafts as quickly as possible (below). A typical escape chute can be used to evacuate 400 to 450 people in less than 30 minutes. Similar chutes are used on airplanes.

"CHUTING" TO SAFETY

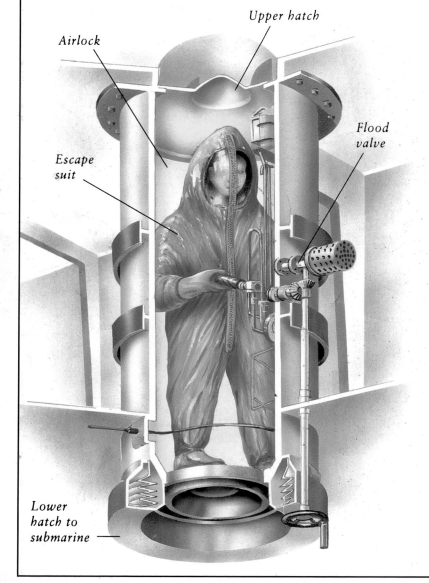

Airlock

Upper hatch

Escape suit

Flood valve

Lower hatch to submarine

ESCAPE TOWER

A submarine escape tower (left *and* right) allows submariners to escape from depths up to 590 ft (180 m) and survive on the surface in freezing conditions.

A SUBMARINER EMERGES

Wearing an insulated and pressurized suit, the crew member enters a floodable airlock that opens to allow them out. Stored in a pocket of the suit is an inflatable life raft, which has a canopy for additional thermal protection.

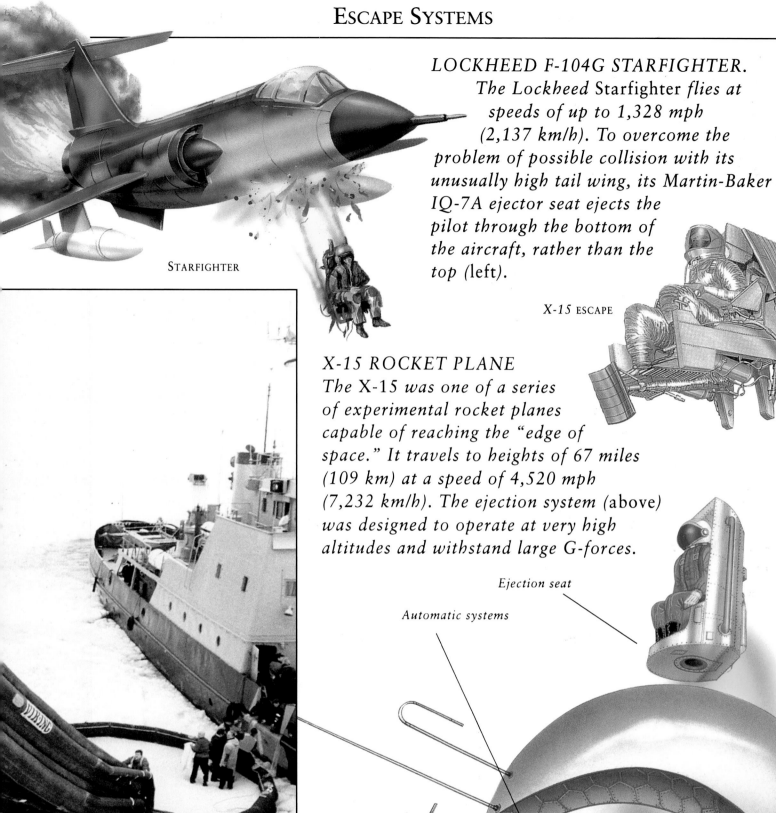

STARFIGHTER

LOCKHEED F-104G STARFIGHTER.
The Lockheed Starfighter flies at speeds of up to 1,328 mph (2,137 km/h). To overcome the problem of possible collision with its unusually high tail wing, its Martin-Baker IQ-7A ejector seat ejects the pilot through the bottom of the aircraft, rather than the top (left).

X-15 ESCAPE

X-15 ROCKET PLANE
The X-15 was one of a series of experimental rocket planes capable of reaching the "edge of space." It travels to heights of 67 miles (109 km) at a speed of 4,520 mph (7,232 km/h). The ejection system (above) was designed to operate at very high altitudes and withstand large G-forces.

Ejection seat

Automatic systems

VOSTOK 1

EJECTING BACK TO EARTH
The Vostok 1 space capsule carried Russian cosmonaut Yuri Gagarin on the first manned space flight in April 1961. Fears that the capsule would not land safely led to Gagarin using the capsule's ejection system and parachuting to Earth after it had reentered the atmosphere (right).

MIR SPACE STATION

FALLING LIKE A STONE

In orbit, the Soyuz rescue craft can be positioned for reentry, but once it enters the Earth's atmosphere, it is difficult to predict where it will land. Friction and drag caused by the atmosphere slow down the craft until the parachutes are deployed. Finally thrusters are fired before touchdown.

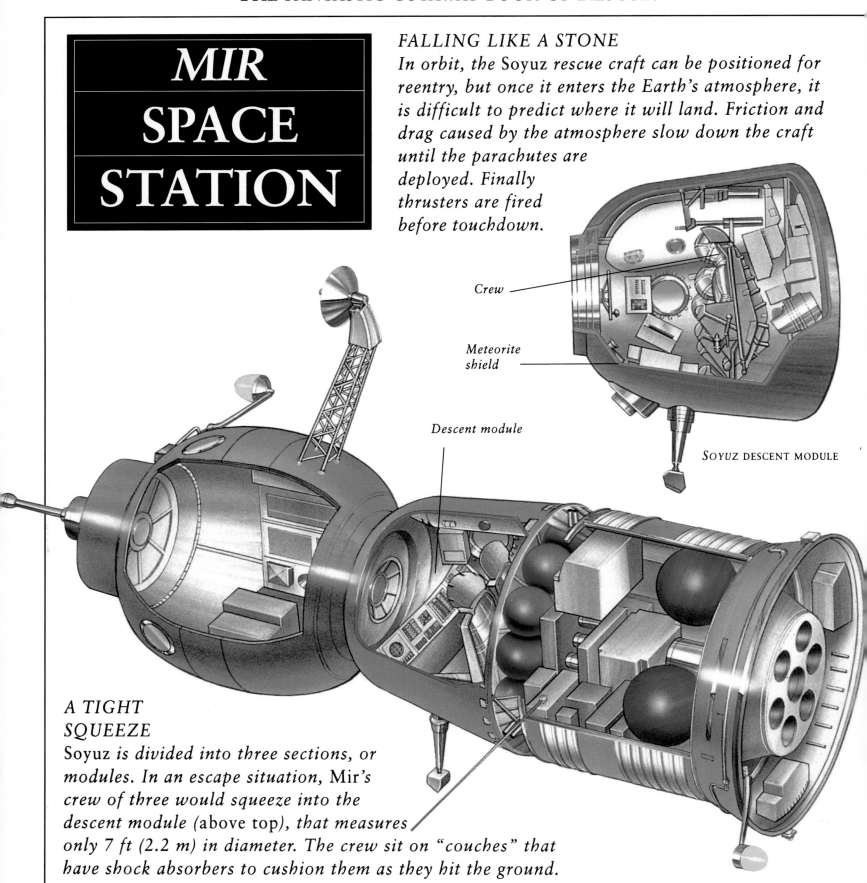

Crew

Meteorite shield

SOYUZ DESCENT MODULE

Descent module

A TIGHT SQUEEZE

Soyuz is divided into three sections, or modules. In an escape situation, Mir's crew of three would squeeze into the descent module (above top), that measures only 7 ft (2.2 m) in diameter. The crew sit on "couches" that have shock absorbers to cushion them as they hit the ground.

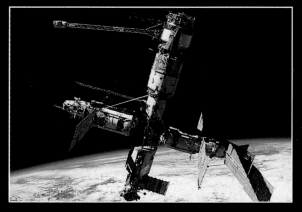

THE *MIR* SPACE STATION

SINCE FEBRUARY 1986, the Russian Space Station *Mir* has been in orbit 250 miles (400 km) above the Earth. Russian cosmonauts have spent record-breaking periods of time in space making space walks and carrying out scientific experiments. The station has suffered a number of serious

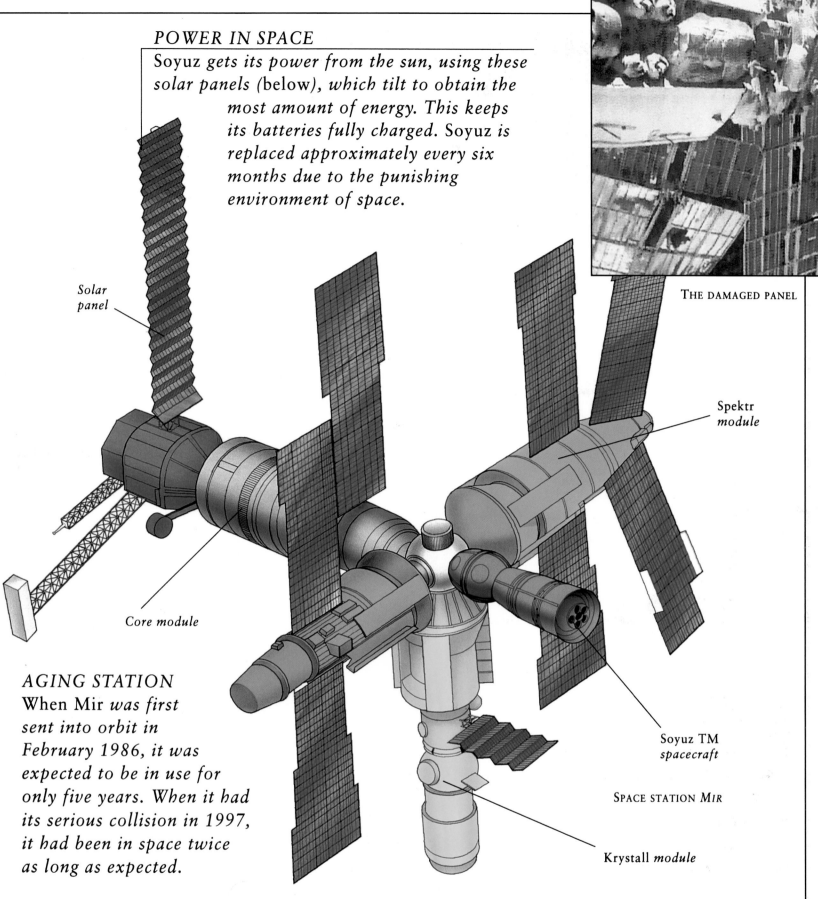

POWER IN SPACE

Soyuz *gets its power from the sun, using these solar panels (below),* which tilt to obtain the most amount of energy. This keeps its batteries fully charged. Soyuz is replaced approximately every six months due to the punishing environment of space.

THE DAMAGED PANEL

Solar panel

Spektr module

Core module

Soyuz TM spacecraft

SPACE STATION MIR

AGING STATION

When Mir *was first sent into orbit in February 1986, it was expected to be in use for only five years. When it had its serious collision in 1997, it had been in space twice as long as expected.*

Krystall *module*

problems, including an onboard fire. In June 1997, the crew nearly had to evacuate the station in the *Soyuz TM* "lifeboat" capsule, when a radio-controlled cargo ship collided with *Mir* during a docking operation. The collision caused the loss of a third of the spacecraft's power supplies, and the air supply in one of *Mir*'s scientific modules, *Spektr*, began falling. *Spektr* had to be sealed off, and cosmonauts had to perform a risky space walk to inspect the damage to the exterior.

RESCUE IN SPACE

*E*mergencies hundreds of miles above the Earth are extremely difficult and expensive to deal with. The most common rescue situations in space involve the repair and retrieval of damaged satellites by the crew of the Space Shuttle (right). The astronauts use an Environmental Mobility Unit to carry out such jobs. Tethered to a remote arm, they carry out their activities with enough oxygen and water to last seven hours. The manufacture of safety systems will be of prime importance, too, as space technology advances with the building of the International Space Station and the possible landing of astronauts on Mars.

Damaged satellite

Work pad

MANNED MANEUVERING UNIT
The Manned Maneuvering Unit (MMU, left) allows an astronaut to carry out activities completely detached from the shuttle orbiter. Its safety system (SAFER) keeps astronauts from "tumbling" out of control, and allows them to jet back to safety.

Remote-control arm

MANNED MANEUVERING UNIT

CREW RETURN VEHICLES

Prototype spacecraft, known as "lifting bodies," as their body shape provides lift (right), are being designed as replacements for the Soyuz capsule, currently used as a lifeboat spaceship (see pages 34-35). Space agencies are developing an emergency Crew Return Vehicle (CRV) for use by cosmonauts on the International Space Station, due in orbit early in the next century. It will be able to carry six passengers, and will steer to practically any landing point on Earth.

A PROTOTYPE "LIFTING BODY"

CHALLENGER DISASTER

In January 1986, the Space Shuttle Challenger *exploded shortly after launching (left). Following this, NASA introduced extra safety measures, such as a crew escape capsule. Air bases around the world are also prepared to receive the shuttle should it need to abort its mission.*

CHALLENGER
EXPLODES

THE APOLLO 13 CREW (FROM THE 1995 FILM)

Aquarius *(lunar module)*

APOLLO 13

Launched in April, 1970, the Apollo 13 mission was to be the third American landing on the Moon. Two days into the mission an oxygen tank exploded, seriously damaging the main service module (right). Facing the prospect of suffocating slowly, the crew were forced to use the Aquarius *lunar module (in which they were due to land on the Moon) as a lifeboat. Its engine was fired to accelerate the module around the Moon and return the crew safely to Earth.*

Damage caused when oxygen tank exploded

Service module

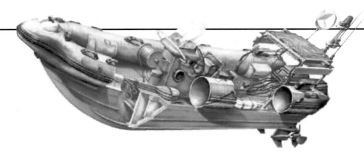

GLOSSARY

Aerodynamic
An aircraft is said to be "aerodynamic" when its shape helps it to travel easily through the air.

Airlock
An airtight compartment with a door at either end. Used to access pressurized chambers, for example in submarines and spacecraft.

Altitude
A measurement of height above sea level.

Closed-Circuit T.V.
A television system used to monitor activity from a distance or in an inaccessible area.

Defibrillator
A device that sends an electric shock through a patient's chest to restart their heart if it has stopped beating.

Drag
A moving object pushes air (or water) forward, causing turbulence behind, which slows down the object. This slowing effect is called drag.

Four-Wheel Drive
Where power is transmitted to all four wheels of a vehicle, to provide extra grip and propulsion.

Friction
A force that works in opposition to the direction an object is going, caused as two surfaces rub over each other.

G-Force
The force that pilots and astronauts experience as they accelerate or decelerate rapidly, and when they turn rapidly; one G represents the ordinary pull of gravity.

Horsepower
The unit of power of an engine, based originally on the power a horse can exert.

Knot
A unit of measurement of a ship's speed, representing one nautical mile per hour, or 1.15 miles (1.85 km).

Module
A section of a vehicle that can be separated from the main part (for example, in spacecraft).

Paramedic
Someone trained to provide medical aid at the scene of an accident and while a patient is being taken to the hospital.

Pressure
A force that presses or squeezes an object.

Propeller
A device with angled blades that rotates to propel a ship through water or an aircraft through the air.

Radar
A system used to detect the position of other objects or vehicles. Short radio waves are sent out and are then measured when they are reflected back again.

Rotor
A part of a machine that rotates (for example, the blades of a helicopter).

Sonar
System that works in a similar way to radar (*see* above), but is used for detecting objects underwater.

Submersible
A vessel capable of working deep beneath the surface of the sea.

Traction
A force used to pull or draw something across a surface.

Transmission
A system of shafts and gearboxes that transmits power produced by an engine to the wheels or propellers of a vehicle.

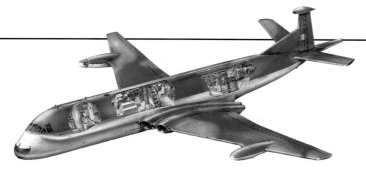

CHRONOLOGY

1487 Horse-drawn carriages used to carry wounded Spanish soldiers become the first ambulances.

1666 The Great Fire of London destroys a large area of the city and encourages the early development of organized firefighting forces.

1715 A diving suit, made of wood and leather, is first used for salvage work.

1736 An early steam-powered tug is built. It is used to move ships into and out of harbors when the wind or tide is against them.

1790 The first lifeboat is designed. It is powered by oars, and has sails for use when conditions are rough.

1800 The first hand-pumped fire engines are used.

1829 The first steam-powered fire engine is built.

1854 The British "National Institution for the Preservation of Life from Shipwreck" becomes the "Royal National Lifeboat Institution" (RNLI).

1864 The Red Cross is formed in Switzerland to aid wounded soldiers in wartime. The organization's symbol, a red cross on a white background, is used today to indicate emergency status.

1899 A prototype motor ambulance is exhibited in Paris.

1902 Motorized ambulances are introduced in Britain.

1930 The first submersible, called a bathysphere, is tested by Americans Otis Barton and William Beebe.

1933 The Australian Aerial Medical Service is established. It is now known as the Flying Doctor Service.

1942 A German test pilot becomes the first to use an ejector seat in an emergency.

1943 The French diver Jacques-Yves Cousteau invents the Aqua-Lung, the first effective independent breathing device.

1944 The first military helicopter rescue mission takes place in Burma (Myanmar) to rescue three British soldiers.

1960 The deep-sea submersible *Trieste* makes the deepest dive ever recorded.

1968 The first successful tests of atmospheric diving suits are carried out, which lead to the development of the Newtsuit.

1970 January The first Deep Submergence Rescue Vehicle is launched, followed by the second in May 1971.

April The Apollo 13 mission to the Moon is aborted after an oxygen tank explodes. The crew are forced to use the thrusters on the lunar lander to power themselves back to Earth.

1985 One of the deepest deep-sea operations, to rescue the flight recorder of a crashed Boeing 747 jet, takes place.

1986 The explosion of the Space Shuttle *Challenger*, killing its crew of seven, leads to a widespread redesign of the space shuttles' emergency procedures.

1988 The Piper Alpha oil rig explodes in the North Sea, killing 167 workers. The disaster prompts changes in platform design, to improve safety.

1993 The Space Shuttle mission succeeds in repairing a fault on the Hubble Space Telescope.

1994 The worst bushfires on record wreak havoc around Sydney, Australia. Bulldozers and excavators stood ready to dig vast fire trenches to halt the advance of the flames and 25,000 people are evacuated.

1997 The Russian Space Station *Mir* experiences a series of problems. At times it seemed likely that they would have to evacuate in the *Soyuz* capsule.

2003 The International Space Station should be completed, using fully reusable "lifeboat" rescue craft.

INDEX

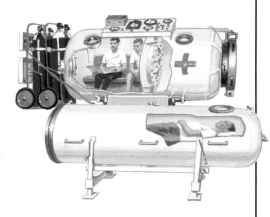

Photographic credits:
Abbreviations t-top, m-middle, b-bottom, r-right, l-left, c-center

Pages 4, 7b, 9tr, 12m, 13, 14 all, 15b both, 17, 19m & br, 20, 25mr, 28tr, 29, 30t, 31, 32-33, 34, 36 & 37mr – Frank Spooner Pictures. 7m, 9m, 12tr, 16, 18 both, 19bl, 25ml, 28tl, 30b, 32t & 37bl – Rex Features. 7 – Shout/911 Pictures. 8 – Hulton Getty Collection. 8 & 9b – Shout Pictures. 10 – London Ambulance Service, NHS Trust. 12tl – Tom Donovan Military Pictures. 15 both – Roger Vlitos. 22 & 32b – Dan Burton Photography. 24t – Mary Evans Picture Library. 24b & 26b – Solution Pictures. 35 – Galaxy Picture Library. 37t – NASA.